Non-Fiction Teacher's Book 2
Irene Yates

Series Editor: Wendy Body
Consultant: Julie Garnett
Written by Irene Yates with additional contribution from Julie Garnett

Pearson Education Limited
Edinburgh Gate
Harlow
Essex
CM20 2JE
England and Associated Companies throughout the World

ISBN 0582 50388 4
First published 2001
Third impression 2002

Printed in China   GCC/03
Designed by AMR, Bramley, Hants

The Publisher's policy is to use paper manufactured from sustainable forests.

Edinburgh Gate
Harlow, Essex

If you wish to enlarge any of the Shared Writing Examples for use in your teaching, you may do so.

Remember that the commentary you give while you are writing is crucial for children's learning, so routinely comment on:

- the spelling of more difficult words

- the sentence punctuation

- why you have chosen certain words

- how you can change your mind and alter things while writing.

Contents

Year 2 Non-Fiction Summary Chart

Text in Resource Book	Text level objective	Sentence level objective links	Unit of work
Term 1 Unit 1 *Our locality*	**T15**: to write simple instructions		Write directions
Term 1 Unit 2 *Our locality* *How to get to the swimming pool by coach* *How to get to the swimming pool on foot*		**S6**: to use a variety of simple organisational devices	Use arrows and boxes
Term 1 Unit 3 *Frog hopping* Writing instructions for a game	**T15**: to write simple instructions		Write instructions for a game
Term 1 Unit 4 *How to make a strawberry smoothie* *Making a smoothie with a different fruit*	**T16**: to use models from reading to organise instructions sequentially		Order instructions in sequence
Term 2 Unit 5 *Candlelight* *How to make a snowman decoration*	**T17**: to use diagrams in instructions		Use diagrams in instructions
Term 2 Unit 6 *Making a den*	**T18**: to use appropriate register in writing instructions		Use appropriate tone for instructions
Term 2 Unit 7 Words from a dictionary Making a simple dictionary	**T20**: to make class dictionaries ... of special interest words, giving ... definitions		Make a dictionary
Term 2 Unit 8 Index from an *Introductory Encyclopaedia of British Wild Animals*	**T20**: to make class dictionaries and glossaries of special interest words ... e.g. linked to topics		Make a glossary

Term 2 Unit 9 Glossary definitions		**S8**: to use commas to separate items in a list	Use commas in lists
Term 2 Unit 10 *Lots of loos*		**S7**: to investigate and recognise a range of other ways of presenting texts	Use captions and headings
Term 2 Unit 11 *Lots of loos*		**S9**: to secure the use of simple sentences in own writing	Write simple sentences
Term 2 Unit 12 *Chicken and egg* *The life of a chicken*	**T21**: to produce simple flow charts or diagrams that explain a process	**S9**: to secure the use of simple sentences in own writing	Draw flow diagrams
Term 2 Unit 13 *Heating and cooling* Making a flow diagram	**T21**: to produce simple flow charts or diagrams that explain a process		Use flow diagrams to explain a process
Term 3 Unit 14 Questions about dinosaurs	**T14**: to pose questions and record these in writing		Write down questions
Term 3 Unit 15 *The last dinosaurs*	**T19**: to make simple notes from non-fiction texts		Make notes from texts
Term 3 Unit 16 *The last dinosaurs* Dinosaur fact file: *Apatosaurus*	**T20**: to write non-fiction texts		Write non-fiction texts
Term 3 Unit 17 Dinosaur fact file: *Apatosaurus*		**S5**: to write in clear sentences using capital letters and full stops	Use capitals and full stops in sentences
Term 3 Unit 18 Fact file: *Indian elephants* Fact file: *African elephants*	**T21**: to write non-chronological reports based on structure of known texts	**S5**: to write in clear sentences using capital letters and full stops	Write a report
Term 3 Unit 19 *Baby clothes*		**S6**: to turn statements into questions	Turn statements into questions
Term 3 Unit 20 *What babies wear today*	**T20**: to write non-fiction texts, using texts read as models … e.g. use of headings, sub-headings		Write non-fiction texts with headings

Introduction

What is *Pelican Shared Writing?*

Pelican Shared Writing is an easy-to-use resource for teaching shared writing. It comprises ten packs: one Fiction and one Non-Fiction pack for each year group for Years 2, 3, 4, 5 and 6. Each pack contains:
- one *Writing Resource Book*
- one *Teacher's Book* with copymasters
- a large sheet of acetate and a Pelican page clip.

Each *Writing Resource Book* offers 20 units of work which cover all the NLS writing composition objectives for the year group. Each writing composition objective forms one unit of work. Links are also made to appropriate sentence level objectives.

Although *Pelican Shared Writing* stands alone, it has links to *Pelican Guided Reading and Writing* in terms of objectives and tasks and there are content links to *Pelican Big Books*.

The *Writing Resource Books*
- Each 48-page big book is split into three parts – one for each term's teaching objectives.
- Shared writing is rooted in shared reading, and so the *Writing Resource Book* contains the texts which not only provide the starting point for writing, but also act as models of the genre to be studied. Story plans and writing frames are sometimes included as well.
- Quotes about the writing process from professional children's writers feature on the inside back cover of some of the *Fiction Writing Resource Books* to initiate discussions on writing.
- Each book comes with a large sheet of acetate and a Pelican page clip for text marking and writing.

The *Teacher's Books*

The *Teacher's Book* in each pack contains:
- teaching pages for each Unit of work with detailed, step-by-step advice on what to do in each shared writing session. There are also examples of completed activities which teachers can use to guide the class in composing a text. Units will usually take more than one shared writing session to complete. Year 2 Units are always split into two sessions.
- a small number of copymasters, e.g. writing frames, character planners. These are for general use and can also be applied to other texts and writing activities.
- copymaster versions of all the *Writing Resource Book* texts. These can be used to make overhead transparencies and in instances where it is helpful for children to have their own copy of a text, e.g. for annotation.

The *Non-Fiction Teacher's Book* has a summary of links to other areas of the curriculum on the last page.

Teaching shared writing

Pelican Shared Writing complements the National Literacy Strategy's *Grammar for Writing* guidance. *Pelican Shared Writing* concentrates on delivering the text level writing composition objectives whereas *Grammar for Writing* concentrates on sentence level objectives. *Pelican Shared Writing* adopts a similar approach to shared writing which may be summarised as follows:

Key features of shared writing
- Make explicit how purpose and audience determine form and style.
- Link the writing to specific objectives.
- Rehearse sentences orally before writing.
- Discuss and explain alternatives and choices.
- Keep re-reading to maintain flow, meaning and consistency.
- Involve children in the revision and editing.

Shared writing techniques

Teacher demonstration

The teacher composes and writes, modelling for children how to compose a particular text type or tackle a writing activity. He/she thinks aloud, rehearses choices before writing, explains choices and makes changes. The children do not contribute to the composition but they are invited to offer opinions on, for example, the choice of words or sentence construction. Demonstration time will vary according to the text and children's competence, but avoid spending too long – children need to try things for themselves.

Teacher scribing

The teacher acts as scribe and builds on the initial demonstration by asking the children to make contributions to the composition or task. The teacher guides, focuses, explains and challenges the contributions, e.g. *Why did you choose that word? That's a really good sentence construction because ...* While children could make their contributions orally by putting up their hands, it is preferable for them to use whiteboards (in pairs or individually), which ensures participation by all children. It is also advisable to take "time out", i.e. children turn to each other in pairs and discuss possibilities for 30 seconds or so.

Supported composition

Supported composition is preparation for independent writing. Children compose a limited amount of text using whiteboards or notebooks – in pairs or individually. Their alternatives are reviewed and discussed and choices and changes made. Some differentiation can be achieved by seating children in their ability groups and asking one group to compose one sentence orally, another to write one or two sentences and a third to write several sentences. Supported composition will enable you to identify those children who will need to repeat or continue the task in guided writing, i.e. those who need greater support.

Shared writing is the most powerful means of improving and developing children's writing skills. But they will not develop into proficient writers unless, firstly, they are given sufficient TIME to practise the skills and craft of writing for themselves, and secondly, they receive the FEEDBACK which will help them evaluate what they have done and learn from it.

Teaching a *Pelican Shared Writing* unit of work

Support for each step will be found on the teaching pages

Discussing the text for each unit
- Introduce the task and the objective.
- Read the text in the Resource Book with the class and discuss the content.
- Draw out features of the genre.

Shared writing
- Demonstrate or model the particular features of the writing.
- Scribe and guide the pupils' contributions.
- Continue with supported composition by children working in pairs.
- Check the children's learning.

Independent writing
- Children complete the writing task.
- They consolidate their learning by carrying out another similar task.

Checking the objective
- Determine children's understanding of the objective and how far they can apply their knowledge by evaluating their writing.

Revisiting the objective
- If necessary, repeat the whole process using the suggested activity.

Note: A *Pelican Shared Writing* CD-ROM is available for use alongside each year's work. For further details, please see the section on ICT overleaf.

ICT and *Pelican Shared Writing*

ICT may be used by all pupils to support writing skills. The word processor or desktop publishing package can enable the child to focus on the development of ideas and the manipulation of the written word without the physical constraints imposed by the handwriting process. The ease of editing, the spell-checking facilities and the ability to move text around the page make ICT support programs valuable tools to include within the writing repertoire. Writing tasks offer the ideal opportunity to integrate and apply those ICT skills being developed in the ICT curriculum.

Almost any writing task may be approached using ICT as an optional writing tool. These writing tasks will offer strong links with the ICT curriculum, which aims that pupils should:

- 'develop their ability to apply their IT capability and ICT to support their use of language and communication'
- 'pass on ideas by communicating, presenting and exchanging information'
- 'develop language skills eg in systematic writing and in presenting their own ideas'
- 'be creative and persistent'
- 'find things out and handle information'
- 'read non-fiction and extract information from sources such as reference books or CD-ROMs.'
- 'recognise the strengths and limitations of ICT'

(*QCA Scheme of Work for ICT, Aims and Purposes*)

The 'Communicating' strand for ICT is inextricably linked with developing literacy. Computer access is a great resource for independent, group and class work, and is too valuable a tool to remain unused during the development of literacy skills. It is a great motivator and encourages collaborative work that can become more focused as children's attention is extended.

Within the suggested Year 2 Non-Fiction *Pelican Shared Writing* activities, there are some clear links with units from the QCA Scheme of Work for ICT, particularly:

- Unit 2C (Finding Information)
- Unit 2E (Questions and Answers)
- Unit 2A (Writing Stories)

Links to the most relevant National Curriculum Programme of Study for ICT are listed in the table opposite.

The differentiated writing frames for Year 2 (Fiction and Non-Fiction) are available on the CD-ROM entitled *Pelican Shared Writing Year 2* (ISBN 0582 50985 8), which can be easily installed on any machine supporting Microsoft Word. Here they may be adapted, should you so wish, to suit your particular needs. The CD-ROM also provides cross-referencing charts for both Writing and ICT targets, including the ICT Programme of Study references and links to the QCA Scheme of Work for ICT – collated and readily available for inclusion in planning records.

Year 2 Non-Fiction
Relevant objectives from the ICT Programme of Study

Pupils should be taught:

1a
to gather information from a variety of sources (*for example, people, books, databases, CD-ROMs, videos and TV*)

1c
to retrieve information that has been stored (*for example, using a CD-ROM, loading saved work*)

2a
to use text, tables, images and sound to develop their ideas

2b
how to select from and add to information they have retrieved for particular purposes

2c
how to plan and give instructions to make things happen (*for example, programming a floor turtle, placing instructions in the right order*)

3a
how to share their ideas by presenting information in a variety of forms (*for example, text, images, tables, sounds*)

3b
to present their completed work effectively (*for example, for public display*)

4a
to review what they have done to help them develop their ideas

4b
to describe the effects of their actions

5b
to explore a variety of ICT tools (*for example, floor turtle, word processing software, adventure game*)

National Curriculum for England, ICT Programmes of Study

Writing objective
T15: To write simple instructions, e.g. getting to school.

Text Copymasters: C7–8

Discussing the text

- Discuss together the 'Our locality' map on Resource Book pages 2 to 3. *What can we see? Which road is the supermarket in? Which road is the cinema in? Where is the Post Office?* etc.
- *Who would like to tell us how we might get from the school to the Post Office? Who could tell us how to get to the supermarket if you lived in Swan Street?* Give individual children a chance to respond with suggestions. Model direct instructional language, e.g. 'You go along …', or 'Turn right at …' etc.
- Explain the task to the children: *Now we are going to **write** directions telling someone how to get from one place to another.*

Shared writing

Session 1
Teacher demonstration

- Give the scenario that your friend has just moved into the West Road flats, behind the school, and she wants to know how to get to the park to walk her dog.
- Talk the children through your chosen route and then write the first instruction (see Shared Writing Example below).

Teacher scribing

- Ask the children to tell you the second part of the directions. Give two or three children the chance to make suggestions.
- Discuss their directions, decide which one works, or put them together to make them work and scribe it.
- Repeat until you have finished the directions.

Shared Writing Example

- Go out of the flats and turn left.
- Cross School Road at the zebra crossing by the Burger bar.
- Walk past the hospital and turn left down East Street.
- Cross East Street at the zebra crossing by the traffic lights.
- Walk past the Post Office and down Swan Street.
- Cross Swan Street at the zebra crossing and you will see the entrance to Swan Park.

Session 2

Teacher scribing

- Recap what the children have learnt about writing directions from Session 1. *What do we need to remember?* Get the directions in the right order. Write clearly. Use short sentences. Use words like 'First' and 'Next', rather than 'and then … and then …' Use 'bossy' words that tell what to do like 'Go along', 'Cross the road'. Use bullet points.
- Choose the start and finish points of a second journey.
- Take suggestions from the children for the first direction and scribe it.

Supported composition

- Ask the children to write the next direction in pairs or individually.
- Check and compare.
- Choose a direction to add to your model and scribe it.

Teacher scribing

- Take suggestions from the children and scribe the next direction.

Supported composition

- Ask the children to write the next direction.
- Alternate scribing and supported composition until the directions are written.

Independent writing

- Give suggestions for journeys. Make this an opportunity for differentiated learning by choosing simple and more complex journeys. Ask the children to write directions for a journey specifically chosen for their level of ability.

Checking children's learning

- Can the children give clear, correct directions orally?
- Can the children write one direction for part of a journey in a simple sentence, correctly punctuated?

Revisiting the objective

- Write the directions for another journey.

Use arrows and boxes

Writing objective

S6: To use a variety of simple organisational devices, e.g. arrows ... boxes ... to indicate sequences.

Text Copymasters: C9–10

Discussing the text

- Explain the task to the children. *We are going to write directions in another way. This time we are going to use boxes and arrows to help us make our directions clear. The arrows will show the order in which you read the directions. The boxes will hold the writing.*
- Check the children's knowledge. *What do we know about directions?* They must be in the right order. They must be clear. They must tell what you do.
- Look at the map together and discuss how to get to the swimming pool from the school. *The journey could be by coach or on foot – this will give two different sets of directions.*
- Ask individual children to give suggestions for routes for each journey. *Which routes are shorter and which are longer? e.g. using the footpath behind the video shop or cutting through the park?*

Shared writing

Session 1
Teacher demonstration

- Use page 4 and the acetate.
- Explain to the children that there is a new coach driver who does not know the town. *We can write directions like a chart.*
- Turn to page 4, read the title and show the children the start and finish points. *We are going to fill in the middle with our directions in words.* Draw the first box.
- Look at the map. Point to the school. *Where does the coach go first? It turns left into School Road ... So I will write 'When you come out of the car park, turn left into School Road' in the first box* (see Shared Writing Example 1).
- *Now I am going to draw an arrow pointing down to the next instruction.* Draw arrow and next box. *The next instruction will go in the second box.*

Teacher scribing

- *What shall I write next, in this box?* Take suggestions from the children and scribe.
- Repeat until the journey is completed.
- Discuss whether it might be clearer to add numbers to the boxes. Do the children think they would be helpful? Add them if agreed.

	Shared Writing Example 1 Driving to the swimming pool	Shared Writing Example 2 Walking to the swimming pool
Start	When you come out of the car park, turn left into School Road.	Use the zebra crossing to cross School Road.
	Turn right up East Street.	Turn right and walk down School Road.
	At the traffic lights, go straight over into Market Street.	Turn left into South Road.
	The swimming pool is the third building on the left. (If you get to the supermarket, you have gone too far!)	After you have passed the Health Centre, turn left into Swan Street.
	Park in the car park behind the building.	Cross Swan Street using the zebra crossing.
		Walk through Swan Park, passing the pond on your left.
Finish		Cross Market Street using the zebra crossing. The swimming pool is opposite. Have a lovely swim!

Session 2
Teacher scribing

- Clip the acetate to page 5.
- Take suggestions for the best route to the swimming pool on foot. *Which do we prefer? Shall we walk through the park or along East Street?*
- Take suggestions from the children for the first instruction and scribe.
- *What do I need to do next?* Draw an arrow and the next box. Take suggestions and scribe (see Shared Writing Example 2).

Supported composition

- Ask the children to follow the steps and write a direction to go in one of the boxes, working in pairs.
- Check and compare. *Is the language direct? Is it a clear, short sentence? Have you started with a capital letter and ended with a full stop?*
- Choose a direction to add to the chart.
- Complete the directions together, scribing for the class.

Independent writing

- The children should use Copymaster C1 to write directions for a return journey. Children may choose whether it is by coach or on foot.

Checking children's learning

- Can the children write clear, accurate directions in chart form?

Revisiting the objective

- Draw 'Start' and 'Finish' points on your board or flipchart. Write directions for another journey. You could use the same map again, or one showing your own locality.

Write instructions for a game

Writing objective
T15: To write simple instructions, e.g. playing a game.

Text Copymasters: C11–14
Discussing the text

- Read through the text 'Frog hopping' on Resource Book pages 6 and 7.
- *What is the text about? What is it doing?* It's about a game, and it's telling us how to play it.
- *So the text gives us 'instructions'. What do we notice about the way it is written?* It has a title and headings for different parts of the instructions. The language is clear so that you can follow the instructions. *We could play the game at break, or in PE, to see if the instructions work.*
- Explain the task to the children, which is to invent a playground game and write instructions for another class to be able to play it. You could use the example given, invent one of your own or use a game that the children know.
- Discuss the chosen game in full.
- Recap the features of instructional text, then show the children the writing frame on pages 8 and 9 and read through it carefully. Ask the children what the headings are for and what they think goes where.
- Read the words in the prompt boxes at the end. *These words are to help us to remember words we could use in our instructions. We can use them to help us to spell and to make sure we get our instructions in the right order.*

Shared writing
Session 1
Teacher demonstration

- Using the acetate, write on page 8 the title the children have chosen for their game.
- Remind the children what the first box is for. *This is where we write a short description of our game.* Look back at page 6, and read the introduction again. Tell the children what you are going to write in the first box (see Shared Writing Example 1) and write it, thinking aloud as you write.
- Move to the 'Getting ready' box. *What have we got to do before we can play the game? I need to draw eggs on the playground so I'll write 'Draw some large egg shapes on the ground'. I'll add 'with chalk' to make it clear.* Write the preparations for the game.

Shared Writing Example 1

Cock-a-doodle doo
A playground game for six or more players. There must be an even number of players.

Getting ready
Draw some large egg shapes on the ground with chalk. Make sure there is lots of space between the eggs.

Choose one person to be the cockerel. The rest are chickens.

Session 2
Teacher scribing

- Read through the beginning of the instructions that were written in Session 1.
- *Where are we now?* We are now at the 'How to play' space.
- Read through the prompt words at the foot of page 9 for cues.
- Take suggestions from the children for the first instruction. Choose one and scribe it (see Shared Writing Example 2).
- Repeat this step with the next two instructions.

Shared Writing Example 2

How to play

- All the chickens run around between the eggs, pecking.
- When the cockerel shouts 'cock-a-doodle doo' all the chickens jump on to the nearest egg.
- Only two chickens are allowed on any one egg. Any chicken who is too late to get on an egg is out.

Supported composition

- Remind the children to look at the prompt words for cues.
- In pairs or individually, ask the children to write the next instruction.
- Check and compare.
- Choose an instruction and scribe.
- Agree how the instructions will end and scribe.

Independent writing

- Discuss another simple game that the children know. Working in pairs, children write instructions for the game, using the frame on Copymasters C13 and C14 (Writing instructions for a game).

Checking children's learning

- Can the children tell you what sort of things should be written under the headings 'Getting ready' and 'How to play'?
- Can the children write simple instructions for playing a playground game?

Revisiting the objective

- Talk through another game that the children all know, e.g. a maths game, and write instructions for it, using the writing frame to structure the writing.

Order instructions in sequence

Writing objective

T16: To use models from reading to organise instructions sequentially, numbering points.

Text Copymasters: C15–16

Discussing the text

*   Look at the text 'How to make a strawberry smoothie' on Resource Book page 10.
*   *This is a special kind of instruction. What is it called?* It is a recipe. *A recipe gives you instructions for making food or a drink.*
*   *What can we see at the beginning?* The heading, which tells us what the recipe is for. Read it. *Who knows what a smoothie is? This next piece of text tells us.* Read it to the children.
*   *What does the first list tell us?* The things that we need. *They are called the ingredients.* Read through the list of ingredients carefully. *What do you notice about the way they are written?*
*   *What does the second list tell us?* What to do. *What do you notice?* The instructions are in order. They are numbered. Each step is shown on a new line. Read the steps to the class. *The instructions tell you what to **do**.* Identify the action words. You may wish to underline them on the acetate, showing that 'Put', Break', 'Add', 'Buzz', 'Taste' and 'Pour' all come at the beginning of the sentence/line.
*   Explain the task to the children, which is to write instructions for making a different kind of fruit smoothie.

Shared writing

Teacher scribing

*   Use the acetate over the writing frame on page 11, 'Making a smoothie with a different fruit'. Refer to the model on page 10 as you write each new sentence.
*   Discuss ideas with the children for what might be needed to make, for example, a banana smoothie. *We'd have to leave out the strawberries and replace them with more bananas. How many bananas? Should we put in some other soft fruit to give it a bit more flavour (like the banana is in the strawberry smoothie)?*
*   *What is the recipe for? What will our heading be?* Write 'Banana', with the children helping you spell it, in the space available.
*   *What do we write next?* A sentence describing what a banana smoothie is like. Make a collaborative decision about the kind of liquid to be added and scribe the description (see Shared Writing Example).
*   *What goes in the first box?* The heading 'Ingredients'. Write the word and underline it.
*   *What do we need? How shall I write the list?* Take suggestions and scribe the list of ingredients.

Shared Writing Example

First the newly laid eggs are put into an incubator.

The baby chick starts to grow.

12 days later most of the yolk has been eaten.

At 19 days the chick has bones, feathers and a hard beak.

Independent writing

Children can either
a) complete the life cycle diagram, using the copymaster, or
b) use the life cycle diagram to explain the development of an invented animal of their own.

Checking children's learning

- Can the children explain what a flow chart is?
- Can the children explain the use of the arrows?

Revisiting the objective

- Using the frames on Copymasters C3 and C4, make a diagram of the life cycle of a dragonfly or a frog.

Writing objective
T21: To produce simple flow charts or diagrams that explain a process.

Text Copymasters: C39–40

Discussing the text

- Check what the children have learned about flow charts. *What is a flow chart? What is it for? What special features does it have?*
- Explain that, although the last flow charts they looked at were cyclical, flow charts do not have to be cycles.
- *This time we are going to make one that doesn't go round in a circle and begin all over again.*
- Read carefully through the text 'Heating and cooling' on Resource Book page 34.

Shared writing

Teacher demonstration

- Show the children the frame on page 35 and read through it, clarifying the terms 'solid' and 'liquid' if necessary.
- Use the acetate to write in the text.
- Explain that you are going to draw a picture with a caption for each stage in the process of heating and cooling chocolate. Refer across to page 34 at each stage of the process.
- *Remember what arrows are used for and where we put them. For the first part of the process I will show a solid piece of chocolate.* Draw a picture of the chocolate.
- *What shall I write for the first stage of the process?* Compose a caption, e.g. 'A bar of chocolate is a solid', verbalising so that the children can understand your thought processes.
- Remind the children about the arrow and draw it in, pointing towards the next stage.

Teacher scribing

- Look at page 34. *What happens when chocolate gets hot? How can we show this as a diagram?* Take suggestions from the children for showing the sun melting the chocolate.
- Take suggestions for a caption. Scribe it. Ask the children to check your punctuation. Show the children how the arrow can be labelled 'HEATING' to indicate the process. The caption shows the result.

Shared Writing Example

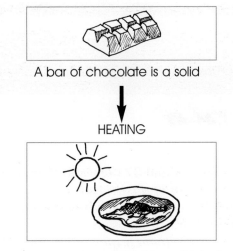

A bar of chocolate is a solid

HEATING

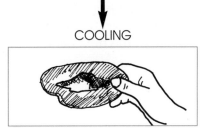

Heat melts the chocolate. It turns it into liquid.

COOLING

Freezing turns the melted chocolate solid again.

Supported composition
- Explain that the next stage is to make the chocolate solid again. *How can this be done? Are there other ways?*
- Ask the children to draw a diagram and write the caption (see Shared Writing Example for an acceptable caption).
- Check, compare and select the most scientifically accurate.
- Choose a diagram and text to add to the shared flow chart.
- *How should we label the arrow? What process turned the chocolate into a solid again?* Cooling. Label the arrow COOLING.
- Finish by discussing why this could not be a cycle diagram even though it starts and finishes with a solid.

Independent writing
- Ask the children to fill in the frame on Resource Book page 35 individually, to explain the process of heating and cooling ice-cream.

Checking children's learning
- Can the children explain to you how a flow chart works?
- Can the children draw and label a simple, clear flow chart?

Revisiting the objective
- Create a flow chart to explain the processes that occur during the cooling and heating of water.

Write down questions

Writing objective
T14: To pose questions and record these in writing.

Text Copymasters: C41–42

Discussing the text

- Look at the picture on pages 36 and 37 ('Questions about dinosaurs'), and discuss it. *Can we identify any of the dinosaurs?*
- Explain the task, which is to compose and write down questions that would lead to information-gathering about dinosaurs.
- *Who can tell me how to write down a question? What do we need to remember?* Write a complete sentence. Make sure there's a question mark at the end.
- *Who can remember six question words?* Why, where, when, who, what, how.
- Have the six question word prompts written on cards and displayed close to the working area, or write them on the flip-chart.

Shared writing

Session 1
Teacher demonstration

- Use the acetate to add questions to the illustrated pages (see Shared Writing Example).
- Before brainstorming ideas for questions the children want to ask about dinosaurs, think of one yourself and demonstrate writing it.
- *What must I make sure of while I'm writing? What must I remember to do – at the beginning of the sentence? At the end?*

Teacher scribing

- Take suggestions from the children for a second question – remind them to look at the prompts to help them, then scribe it.
- *Have we remembered to make it a complete sentence? Have we remembered the question mark? Have we spelled our question word correctly?*

Shared Writing Example

When were the dinosaurs living on earth?

Where did dinosaurs live?

How did the dinosaurs move?

What was the smallest/largest dinosaur called?

Supported composition

- Reminding the children that they are *asking* questions, not answering them, at this stage, give them time out in pairs to choose another question to write.
- Check for correct punctuation and sense.
- Choose one question to add to the model.

Session 2
Teacher scribing

- Recap the work done in the last session and read through the questions written down so far.
- Remind the children of the question prompts on the cards.
- Take suggestions for another question. *What have we got to remember when we write the question down?* It has to be a complete sentence. It has to start with a capital letter and have a question mark at the end.

Supported composition

- Ask the children to write a further two questions. Make this an opportunity for differential learning by giving particular groups of children specific prompt words with which to frame their questions, e.g. more able children to *'Ask a 'why' question'*.

Independent writing

- Children write questions for each other, swap boards and write answers.

Checking children's learning

- Can the children tell you six ways to frame a question?
- Can the children tell you how a written question is punctuated?
- Can the children think up and write a simple question?

Revisiting the objective

- Frame a set of questions around your current classroom topic (using Copymaster C6 if required) and write them down as part of a display.

Make notes from texts

Writing objective
T19: To make simple notes from non-fiction texts.

Text Copymasters: C43–45

Discussing the text

- Read through the whole of 'The last dinosaurs' on Resource Book pages 38 to 40.
- Explain the task, which is to make notes about one of the dinosaurs in order to turn them into a fact file in a future session.
- Explain what notes are and why they are useful.
- Discuss and choose which dinosaur you will make notes on.
- *Before we write our notes, it helps to read the text and underline the most important words.*

Shared writing

Session 1
Teacher demonstration

- Use the acetate to underline key facts.
- Read through the report again.
- Look at the text relating to the Torosaurus. *What is the first important fact? I think we need to note that …* Underline your first key fact, e.g. 'plant eating' (see Shared Writing Example 1). *Now we need to look for the next important fact and underline it …* Underline the next fact.
- Repeat for as long as you feel is necessary.

Teacher scribing

- Continue reading the text and underlining, asking for children's suggestions and discussing which words are unimportant and which are important.

Shared Writing Example 1

The Torosaurus was a <u>plant eating</u> dinosaur that usually <u>lived in a herd</u>. It had the <u>largest head</u> of any dinosaur, with an <u>enormous crest</u> to frighten away meat eaters. It had <u>huge horns to defend itself</u>, and a <u>heavy beak to tear down branches or dig up roots</u>. It had <u>flat teeth to grind up its food</u>. A fully grown Torosaurus <u>could weigh seven tonnes</u>.

Session 2
Teacher scribing

- Recap the work done in the last session.
- *Now we are going to write the facts that we have underlined as a list. They will be our notes. We don't have to use complete sentences, we just use words or phrases. What shall we write first?* Write the name of the chosen dinosaur and underline it.
- *What will our first note be?* Write the first underlined fact, e.g. 'Plant eating' (see Shared Writing Example 2).
- *The next note will go underneath. This will make a list of notes, which is easy to read.*
- Take suggestions for the following notes and scribe them. Discuss whether they are easy to understand or whether extra words should be added.

Shared Writing Example 2

Torosaurus notes –

Plant eating

Lived in herds

Largest head of all dinosaurs

Enormous crest for frightening other dinosaurs

Huge horns for defence

Heavy beak for tearing and digging

Flat teeth for grinding

Weighed seven tonnes

Supported composition
- Reminding them to make a vertical list, ask the children to write the last three notes on their whiteboards.
- Check and compare.
- Choose three notes to add to the shared list.

NB: These notes should be kept for the next writing unit.

Independent writing
- Children make a list of the three facts they think are the most interesting or important.

Checking children's learning
- Can the children explain one way of extracting notes and writing them down?

Revisiting the objective
- Make notes on the Tyrannosaurus Rex in the same way (see Resource Book page 40).

Write non-fiction texts

Writing objective
T20: To write non-fiction texts, using texts read as models for own writing.

Text Copymaster: C46

Discussing the text

- Read the notes made in the last session.
- Read the fact file on the Apatosaurus on page 41.
- Explain the task, which is to use the notes to produce a fact file on their chosen dinosaur, using the fact file on page 41 as a model.
- Examine how the fact file is structured, drawing attention to: the sub-headings (read each one in turn); the language – *It is written like the notes we made – not in complete sentences.*

Shared writing

Session 1
Teacher demonstration

- *First, we need to write the main heading, giving the name of our dinosaur.* Demonstrate writing the heading and add phonetic pronunciation in brackets as on page 41.
- Discuss presentation and layout of your shared fact file. *Do we need to show what the dinosaur looked like?* Leave room for an illustration. Write the sub-headings under each other, spaced out down the left-hand side of the board.
- *The first sub-heading is 'Appearance'. What shall I write there?* Read through the notes, identifying and writing those that relate to the dinosaur's appearance. Verbalising your thought processes, compose and write in all the facts about its appearance.

Teacher scribing

- Take suggestions from the children for what to write for 'Weight' and scribe.

Session 2
Teacher scribing

- Recap the work completed in the last session. If necessary, re-read the fact file on page 41 and the shared notes again.
- Take suggestions from the children on what to write for 'Food' and scribe.

Shared Writing Example

Dinosaur fact file – Torosaurus (pronounced tor-oe-sor-us)

Appearance: Large head with enormous crest. Huge horns and heavy beak

Weight: Up to 7 tonnes

Food: Plants

How it lived: In herds, tearing down branches, digging up roots

Interesting facts: Had the largest head of all the dinosaurs

Supported composition
- Read the next sub-heading. Re-read the notes together.
- Children write the sub-heading 'How it lived' and the content on their whiteboards.
- Check and compare. *What facts did you include? Have you written complete sentences? Have you written in note form?*
- Choose text to add to the shared fact file.

Independent writing
- The children research, make notes and write a fact file on a chosen dinosaur for a class book on dinosaurs. This could be a paired activity.

Checking children's learning
- Can the children tell you what headings and sub-headings are?
- Can the children write the heading and sub-headings for a fact file?

Revisiting the objective
- Write a fact file on the Tyrannosaurus Rex, using the one on page 41 as your model.

Use capitals and full stops in sentences

Writing objective
S5: To write in clear sentences using capital letters and full stops accurately.

Text Copymaster: C46

Discussing the text

- Read through the text on Resource Book page 41.
- Explain the task, which is to turn the fact file into a report. *We are going to write the information in the fact file again, but this time in full sentences so that it makes a report. We need to write in complete sentences, using capital letters and full stops.*

Shared writing

Session 1
Teacher demonstration

- First demonstrate writing the heading.
- Look at the first fact sub-headed 'Appearance'. Explain to the children that you are going to turn the notes into complete sentences so you will need to add words.
- Thinking aloud, compose and write one or two sentences using the information given, e.g. *'One of the largest land animals ever.' Shall I write 'It was ...' or 'The Apatosaurus was ...'? As it is the opening sentence I will write 'The Apatosaurus was ...'* (see Shared Writing Example 1).

Teacher scribing

- Reminding the children of the capital letters and full stops, take suggestions for the second piece of information about its appearance and scribe it.
- Repeat with the third fact about appearance.

Shared Writing Example 1

The Apatosaurus

The Apatosaurus was one of the largest land animals that ever lived. It could sometimes be as much as 27 metres long and 15 metres tall. It had a long neck and tail. Its nostrils were on the top of its head.

Session 2
Teacher scribing

- Re-read the beginning of the report about the Apatosaurus and compare with the fact file.
- Read the fact file items about weight and food. Take suggestions for changing these into complete sentences. Discuss whether they could be combined into one. Try different ways. Scribe the agreed sentence/s (see Shared Writing Example 2).

Shared Writing Example 2

It was a plant eater and could weigh up to 35 tonnes.

Supported composition

- Ask the children to choose one of the three facts under the sub-heading 'How it lived'. Give them time to rehearse their sentence with a partner and then write it as a sentence on their whiteboards – *Remember the capital letters and full stops*.
- Check for sense and punctuation.
- Choose three interesting, correct sentences to add to the shared report.

Independent writing

- Ask the children to swap the fact files they wrote independently in an earlier session and write the facts in the form of a report, using complete sentences and illustrating it.

Checking children's learning

- Can the children tell you what makes a complete sentence?
- Can children write a *clear*, correctly punctuated sentence?

Revisiting the objective

- Using the model fact file format, write up some facts about another dinosaur and then change them into sentences to add to the class dinosaur book.

Writing objective

T21: To write non-chronological reports based on the structure of known texts.

Text Copymasters: C43–45 and C47–48

Discussing the text

- Explain the task, which is to write a report about elephants.
- *Let's look at a report in this book. It's one we have already read.* Read through the dinosaur report on pages 38 to 40.
- Now read the elephant fact files on pages 42 and 43.
- Discuss the information contained in the fact file. *How does it tie in with the report on the dinosaurs?* There are two kinds of dinosaurs and two kinds of elephants.
- *What does the first part of the dinosaur report do?* It tells about one kind of dinosaur. *What does the second part do?* It tells about the other kind. *This is like the fact file on elephants. First it tells about Indian elephants, then it tells about African elephants.*

Shared writing

Session 1
Teacher demonstration

- *If we look at the opening paragraph of the dinosaur report – the introduction – it will give us some idea of how to begin the elephant report.*
- Read through the introduction. Look at the elephant fact file for a general topic of introduction for the elephant report.
- Thinking aloud as you go, compose and demonstrate writing your introductory paragraph (see Shared Writing Example 1). *Remember we are writing in complete sentences, using capital letters and full stops.*

Shared Writing Example 1

Elephants

There are two kinds of elephants living in the wild. These are Indian elephants, which live in South-east Asia, and African elephants, which live in Africa, south of the Sahara Desert.

Teacher scribing

- *What shall we write next?* Look at the dinosaur report and read the paragraph headed 'The Torosaurus' again. Read through the facts on the Indian elephant. *How can we write a paragraph to compare with the paragraph on the Torosaurus?*
- *What will our sub-heading be?* Write the heading 'Indian elephants'.
- Look at the information about the elephant's appearance. *How can we write the first three facts in one sentence?* Give the children time out to compose a sentence with a partner (see Shared Writing Example 2).

- Take suggestions from the children and scribe, reminding the children about the rules of sentences, including commas in lists, as you go along.
- Repeat the last step until you reach 'Other interesting facts'.

Shared Writing Example 2

Indian elephants

Indian elephants have rough grey skin, a long trunk and small ears. The male elephants have tusks. They grow to 3 metres high, and weigh about $5\frac{1}{2}$ tonnes. They eat grass, leaves, fruit and bark. They drink by sucking water up their trunks and shooting it down their throats. They work in the forests, pulling and carrying loads of timber. They are also used in special processions.

Supported composition
- Ask children to write one final sentence giving the interesting fact. Remind them that they are writing about 'elephants' not 'an elephant'.
- Check and compare. How did children join the two pieces of information? Did anyone use 'which' rather than 'and'?
- Choose a sentence, or combine two sentences, to add to your text.

Session 2
Teacher scribing
- Recap the work completed in the last session. Remind the children that they are writing a report.
- Read through the sentences written so far.
- Read through the fact file again, making sure that you have covered all the information on the Indian elephant.
- *What will our next sub-heading be?* Write the heading 'African elephants'.
- Take suggestions from the children for two sentences about what African elephants look like. Scribe them with the children supplying the punctuation.

Supported composition
- Ask the children to write one sentence about the height and weight of African elephants. Remind them about writing in the plural. You could supply a sentence starter, e.g. 'Adult African elephants …'
- Check and compare.
- Choose a sentence to add to the report.

Independent writing
- Ask the children to complete the report.

Checking children's learning
- Can the children explain what a report is?
- Can they tell you some of the features of report writing?

Revisiting the objective
- Research and make a fact file for a further species of animal using the one on page 41 as your model, then write it up as a report.

Turn statements into questions

Writing objective

S6: To turn statements into questions, learning a range of 'wh' words typically used to open questions.

Text Copymasters: C49–52

Discussing the text

- Read 'Baby clothes' on Resource Book pages 44 to 47.
- Talk about the babies' and toddlers' clothing. *How does it compare with what babies and toddlers wear today?*
- Explain the task, which is to turn statements into questions and write them down. *Let's pretend that another class is doing a topic on clothes babies and toddlers used to wear. We are going to use this information to work out some questions for them as a guide.*
- *What is a statement? It does not ask, it tells. Information books contain lots of sentences that are statements. They state facts about the topic.* Read out a sentence from page 44 as an illustration.
- *What do we know about questions?* They ask something. When they are written, they must be complete sentences. When they are written, they end with a question mark. Remind the children of the six question prompts – why, when, where, what, who, how.

Shared writing

Session 1
Teacher demonstration

- Using the text on pages 44 and 45, use the acetate to underline the statements. Read a sentence at a time and ask of each: *Is this a question or a statement?* Underline each statement, i.e. all the sentences!
- Now re-read each statement on page 44 in turn, rephrase them aloud as questions and write them on your board (see Shared Writing Example 1), thinking the punctuation and grammar aloud as you go.

Shared Writing Example 1 (page 44)

When were our grandparents babies?
What did small babies wear in the 1950s?
How were babies' nighties fastened?
What sort of nappies did babies wear in the 1950s?
What were they made of?

Teacher scribing

- Repeat for the first two sentences on page 45 and the photo caption, this time devising questions collaboratively and scribing for the class. See Shared Writing Example 2.

Supported composition

- Looking at the last sentence on page 45, give the children time out to rehearse a question with a partner and then write it on their whiteboards.
- Check and compare.
- Choose a question to add to the model. For example, 'What colours were baby clothes in the 1950s?'

Session 2
Teacher scribing

- Recap the work in the last session.
- Check the children's knowledge about statements and questions. Check the children's knowledge of 'wh' words for asking questions.
- Take suggestions from the children for turning the heading on page 46 into a question and scribe it, reminding the children about how questions are written.
- Take suggestions for turning the first two sentences and the caption into questions and scribe them. See Shared Writing Example 3.

Supported composition

- Ask the children to rehearse with a partner and then write down as many questions as they can create from the information given on page 47.
- Check and compare all the questions.
- Choose questions to add to your model.

Independent writing

- Children write three or four more questions about the lives of their grandparents as babies and toddlers.

Checking children's learning

- Can the children tell you key differences between a written statement and a written question?
- Can the children write a question, correctly punctuated, about babies or toddlers?

Revisiting the objective

- Write some more statements about life in the 1950s. Turn them into questions.

Write non-fiction texts with headings

Writing objective

T20: To write non-fiction texts, using texts read as models for own writing, e.g. use of headings, sub-headings.

Text Copymasters: C49–53

Discussing the text

- Read through the writing frame on Resource Book page 48 'What babies wear today'.
- Keeping in mind the information from the text on pages 44 and 45, discuss the kind of clothing that babies wear today.
- Explain the task to the children, which is to write a report on babies' clothing, using the writing frame to help, and using the text pages as a model. Look at the model and discuss what you need to include to support the text, i.e. heading/s, labelled illustrations and photographs (ideally) with captions.

Shared writing

Session 1
Teacher demonstration

- Look at the first paragraph starter on the writing frame.
- Return to the text and read through the first two sentences.
- Decide, with the children, what babies wear now instead of long nighties. *What are the new garments called? What do they look like? What are they made of? How do they fasten?*
- Thinking aloud as you write, compose and write two or three sentences on the lines of the first two sentences of the model text. Focus on tense agreement, i.e. *Do I write 'These were' or 'These are'?* Re-read aloud, from 'Small babies today wear ...'
- *Do we need an illustration here? What of?* Note 'drawing of baby gro captioned "baby gro" and with label "poppers for changing nappy easily"'.
- Look at the second starter and the third sentence of the text. Decide on a comparable item of clothing, e.g. disposable nappies (see Shared Writing Example 1). Verbalising your thought processes, compose and write a sentence. Make a note of what nappy illustration or diagram you want here.

Teacher scribing

- Look at the third starter and the first and second sentences on page 45.
- Take suggestions from the children for composing and writing comparable sentences.

Supported composition

- Discuss the colours of modern baby clothes. Ask the children to complete the last sentence starter on the frame, using the last sentence in the text as their model.
- Check and compare.
- Choose a sentence to add to the shared writing.

Session 2
Teacher scribing

- Recap the work done in the last session.
- Look at the writing frame on Copymaster C5.
- Look at the text on pages 46 and 47.
- Remind the children that the text is a model or guide, and the prompts on the Copymaster help to start the sentences. There are also helpful words at the bottom of the page to suggest ideas and support spelling.
- Take suggestions for completing 'Boy toddlers wear …' and scribe the sentence or sentences. See Shared Writing Example 2.

Supported composition

- Remind the children again about the prompts and the model text.
- Ask the children to complete the section starting 'Girl toddlers wear …'
- Check and compare.
- Choose sentences to add to your own text.
- Discuss illustrations with captions or labels that might be added.

Independent writing

- Children complete the toddler frame.

Checking children's learning

- Can the children explain how they wrote the report on what babies wear?
- Can the children write a simple information text that includes: a heading; several clear sentences in the present tense; illustrations with captions or labels?

Revisiting the objective

- Write an information text about what adults wear today.

Start

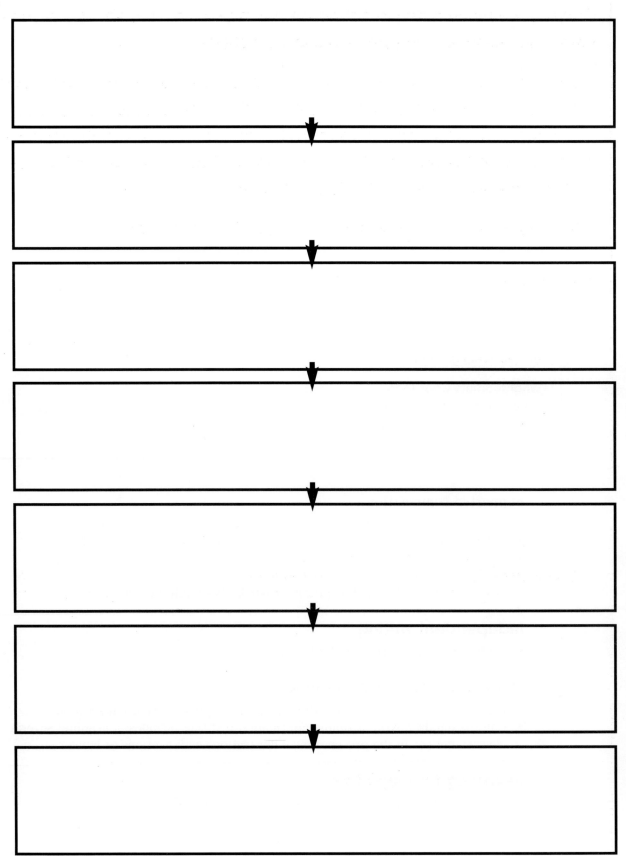

Finish

One day we made a den in our house. Mum let us have a sheet and some towels and cushions and we also used the chairs.

We put the chairs in the corner so that it made a square with the door and the wall. We made the roof first. We stretched the sheet across the top and poked the ends down behind the chairs. Next, we put most of the towels on the floor inside the den. We kept one to make a door with. We put all the cushions inside and pretended to go to sleep.

When Mum came to find us she had to knock on our towel door.

Instructions

What you need

What you do

The life cycle of a dragonfly

C3

The dragonfly lays its eggs in a pond in early autumn. When the weather gets cold, the dragonfly dies. The dragonfly eggs stay in the water during winter. They will not start to hatch into nymphs until the warm weather arrives in spring. When the nymph hatches out it will feed on water fleas, tadpoles and small fish. The adult dragonfly eventually hatches from the nymph, leaving a dry case behind it.

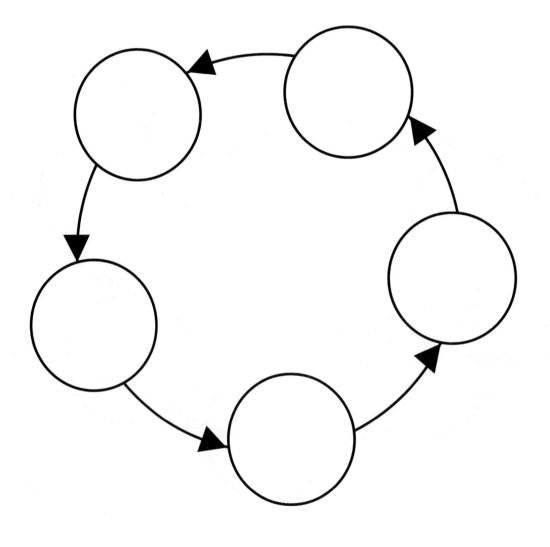

A female frog lays up to 3000 eggs at a time. The mass of eggs is called frogspawn. It sinks to the bottom of the pond and then floats to the surface. Tadpoles hatch from the spawn in late May. They grow back legs first, then front legs. They slowly lose their tails and become young frogs. If they are not eaten, the young frogs sit in the sun and catch flies for food.

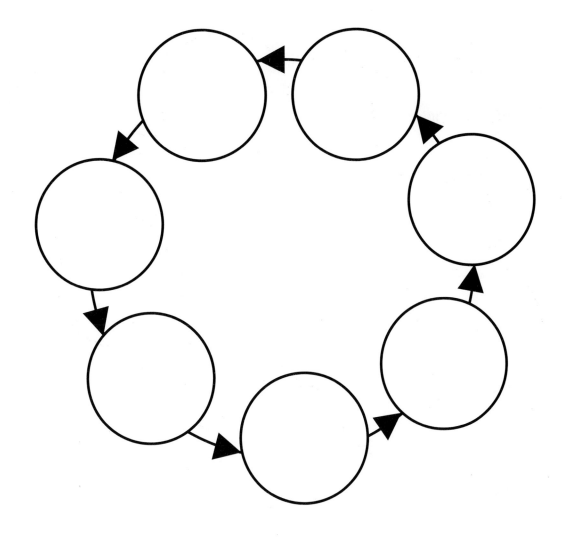

Boy toddlers wear

Girl toddlers wear

Outside, toddlers wear

Most toddler clothes today are

Helpful words:

jeans   joggers   tights   leggings   tops   jumpers
trainers   boots   sandals   wellies   macs   shorts
jog-suits   T-shirts   fleeces   jackets   dungarees

bright   colourful   trendy   hard-wearing   easy-care
easily washed   elasticated   fleecy   cotton   polyester   denim

Our topic is all about

We have learned that

We know that

Our information tells us

Another fact we have learned is that

We still need to find out about

These are questions we could ask to find out more:

Our locality

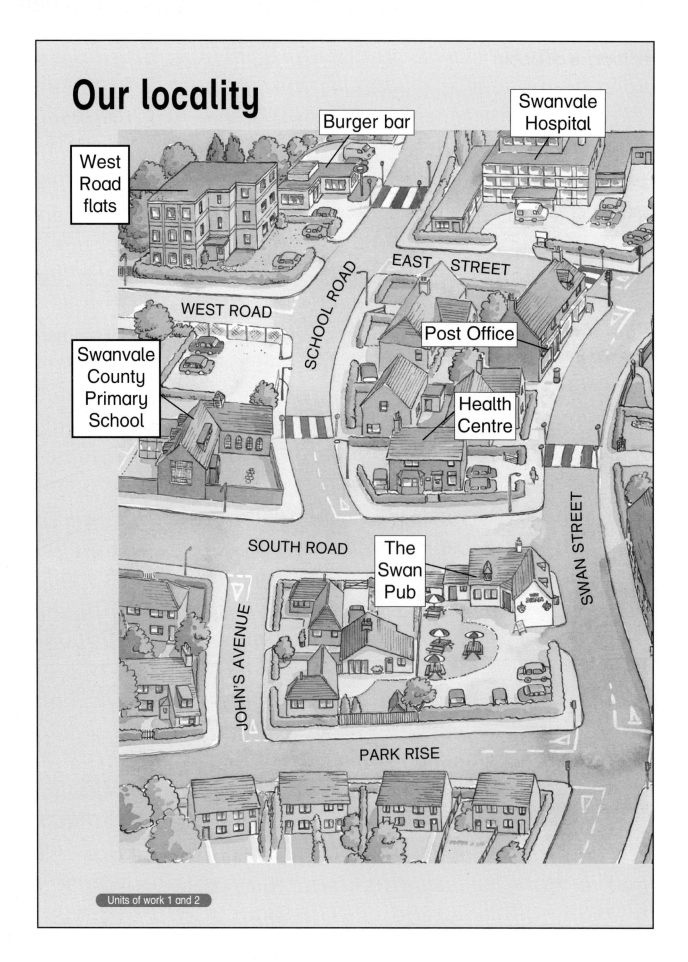

Burger bar

Swanvale Hospital

West Road flats

Swanvale County Primary School

Post Office

Health Centre

WEST ROAD

SCHOOL ROAD

EAST STREET

SWAN STREET

SOUTH ROAD

The Swan Pub

JOHN'S AVENUE

PARK RISE

Islamic Centre

Video shop

Footpath

Swimming pool

Supermarket

SWAN STREET

All Saints Church

Swan Park

MARKET STREET

Sweet shop

Petrol station

Cinema

PARK RISE

Park Rise flats

How to get to the swimming pool by coach

START

FINISH

Units of work 1 and 2

How to get to the swimming pool on foot

START

FINISH

Units of work 1 and 2

Frog hopping

A playground game, suitable for six or more players. There must be an even number of players.

Getting ready

Use chalk to draw a few large lily pads on the playground. Make sure there are big spaces in between them for the 'pond'. Choose one person to be Big Frog.

Unit of work 3

How to play

- Everyone should run around in any direction between the lily pads.

- When Big Frog croaks 'birrit', 'birrit', jump on to a lily pad.

- Only two 'frogs' are allowed on a lily pad. Anyone left in the 'pond' is out.

- After each round of the game, put a bean bag on a lily pad to show it cannot be used.

- The winners are the two children left on the last lily pad.

Writing instructions for a game

Getting ready

How to play

run   chase   shout   stop   go
hop   turn   touch   jump

first   second   next   now
then   after   finally   last

How to make a strawberry smoothie

Smoothies are refreshing fruity drinks made with milk and yoghurt or cream.

Ingredients (makes 3 large glasses)

- 1 banana
- 16–20 strawberries (washed)
- 250ml of milk
- 3 tablespoons yoghurt
- 2 tablespoons runny honey

What to do

1 Put the strawberries in a food mixer or liquidiser.
2 Break the banana into three and add.
3 Add the milk, yoghurt and honey.
4 Buzz until smooth.
5 Taste. If it is too thick, add more milk.
6 Pour into glasses and drink. Mmmmmm!

Unit of work 4

Making a smoothie with a different fruit
How to make a _____ smoothie

-
-
-
-
-

1

Pelican Shared Writing Non-Fiction Year 2 © Pearson Education Limited 2001

Candlelight
How to make a candle decoration for Divali or Christmas

You will need:
- a piece of paper 12cm x 8cm
- scissors
- a gold felt pen or gold glitter
- felt pens or wax crayons

What to do:

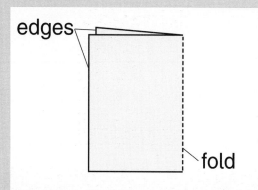

edges

fold

1 Fold the paper in half longways.

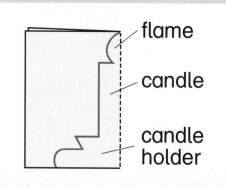

flame

candle

candle holder

2 Draw half a candle shape along the fold.

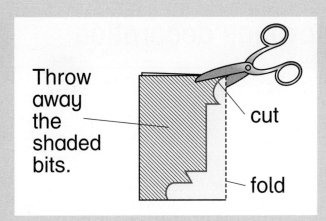

Throw away the shaded bits.

cut

fold

WARNING Do not cut along the fold.

3 Cut along the line you have drawn.

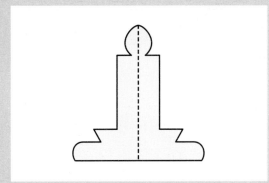

4 Open out the candle.

5 Colour the flame gold with felt pen or glitter.

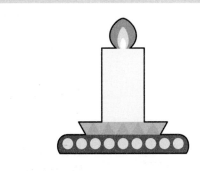

6 Decorate the candle holder with felt pens or crayons.

7 Display your candle in a window or on a wall.

Unit of work 5

How to make a snowman decoration

You will need:

What to do:

1.

2.

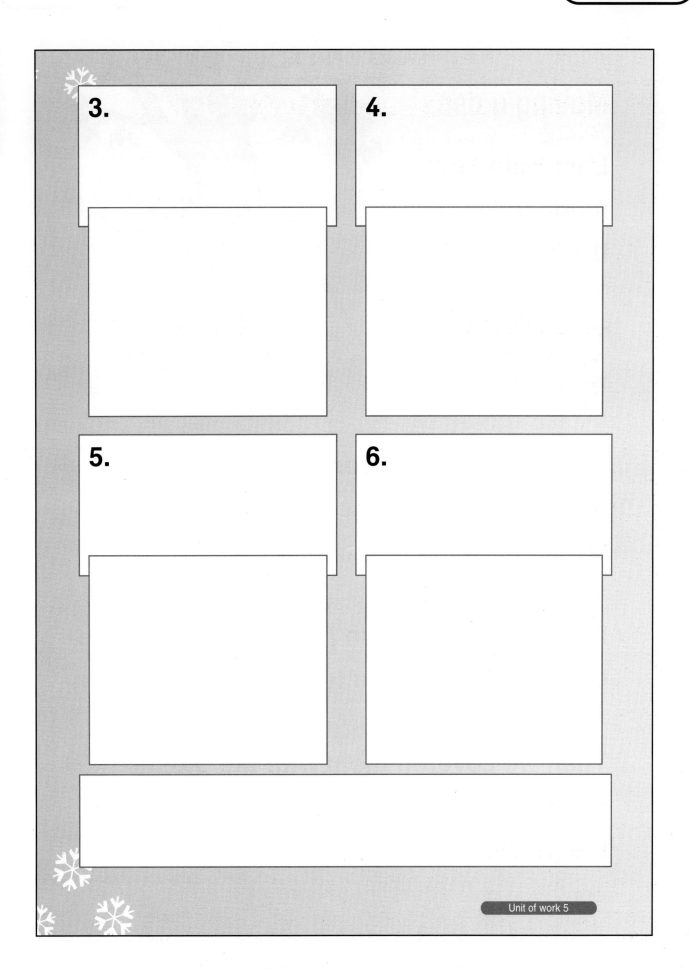

3.

4.

5.

6.

Unit of work 5

Making a den

Last week we made a den at the bottom of Tom's garden. This is how we made it.

We got some old bean poles off Tom's dad, a big plastic sheet and a bit of old carpet from my mum.

First we put the bean poles up against the old apple tree, like a tent.

Then we covered them with the plastic sheet and tucked it under both ends of the poles.

Unit of work 6

We left a gap for the entrance (Tom's cat went in through it) and we had a flap of plastic for the door. We put the carpet down on the floor inside. We had a picnic in there and when it rained we didn't get wet. We want to sleep in there in the summer when it's warm.

Pelican Shared Writing Non-Fiction Year 2 © Pearson Education Limited 2001

ape–bee

Words from a dictionary

ape
a big
monkey

ark
Noah's
floating home

ash
dust that is left when
something burns up

ball
a round thing for
throwing or hitting

bee
a buzzing
insect

Unit of work 7

blade
the sharp
part of a knife

blue
the colour
of the sky

boil
to heat water
until it bubbles

cot
a baby's bed

cow
an animal that
gives us milk

Unit of work 7

crust–dog

Making a simple dictionary

crust

cub

cuff

dog

down

dress

duck

ear

eat

Unit of work 7

Index from an *Introductory Encyclopaedia of British Wild Animals*
A–C

Adder	reptile	2
Ant	insect	3
Badger	mammal	4
Bat	mammal	5
Blackbird	bird	6
Bluebottle	insect	7
Blue tit	bird	8
Bumble bee	insect	9
Butterfly	insect	10
Cod	fish	11
Crab	crustacean	12
Cranefly	insect	13
Cricket	insect	14
Crow	bird	15
Cuckoo	bird	16

Units of work 8 and 9

Pelican Shared Writing Non-Fiction Year 2 © Pearson Education Limited 2001

Index D–L

Deer	mammal	18
Dragonfly	insect	19
Earwig	insect	20
Fox	mammal	21
Frog	amphibian	22
Grass snake	reptile	23
Gull	bird	24
Hare	mammal	25
Hedgehog	mammal	26
Jay	bird	27
Kestrel	bird	28
Kingfisher	bird	29
Ladybird	insect	30
Limpet	mollusc	31
Lizard	reptile	32

Units of work 8 and 9

Index M–R

Magpie	bird	34
Mole	mammal	35
Mosquito	insect	36
Moth	insect	37
Mouse	mammal	38
Mussel	mollusc	39
Newt	amphibian	40
Otter	mammal	41
Owl	bird	42
Oyster	mollusc	43
Pike	fish	44
Pond skater	insect	45
Rabbit	mammal	46
Rat	mammal	47
Robin	bird	48

Units of work 8 and 9

Index S–Z

Shrimp	crustacean	50
Slow worm	reptile	51
Slug	mollusc	52
Snail	mollusc	52
Sparrow	bird	54
Spider	arachnid	55
Squirrel	mammal	56
Starling	bird	57
Stickleback	fish	58
Swan	bird	59
Swift	bird	60
Thrush	bird	61
Toad	amphibian	62
Vole	mammal	63
Wagtail	bird	64
Wasp	insect	65
Water spider	arachnid	66
Weasel	mammal	67
Woodlouse	crustacean	68
Woodpecker	bird	69

Units of work 8 and 9

Glossary definitions

A mammal is a warm blooded animal with a backbone. Female mammals are able to feed their babies with milk.

Crustaceans are animals which have a hard shell and jointed legs.

Reptiles are cold blooded animals with dry scaly skin. They lay eggs.

Insects are small and sometimes have wings. They always have six legs.

Units of work 8 and 9

Pelican Shared Writing Non-Fiction Year 2 © Pearson Education Limited 2001

A bird is an animal that has wings and feathers. All birds lay eggs and nearly all birds can fly.

An arachnid is an animal which has four pairs of legs.

Molluscs have soft bodies with no backbone. Some (like snails) have a shell but some (like slugs) have no shell.

An amphibian is an animal which can live in water or on land.

Lots of loos

Units of work 10 and 11

Units of work 10 and 11

Chicken and egg

1

This egg is being put into an incubator to keep it at just the right temperature.

2

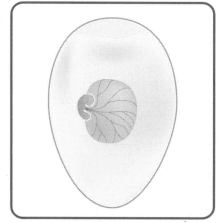

Inside the egg a baby chick starts to grow, using the yolk for food.

3

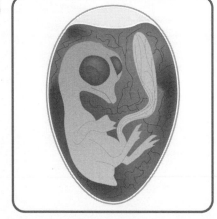

After 12 days most of the yolk has been used up.

4

After 19 days feathers and bones have developed. The beak is hard enough for the chick to use to break the shell.

Unit of work 12

5

Three weeks after they were laid, the eggs hatch. The chicks are covered with fluffy yellow feathers.

6

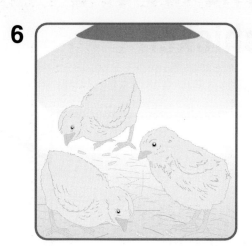

For the first three or four weeks the chicks must be kept warm.

7

After 18 weeks the chicks have become full grown hens. They are now old enough to start laying.

Unit of work 12

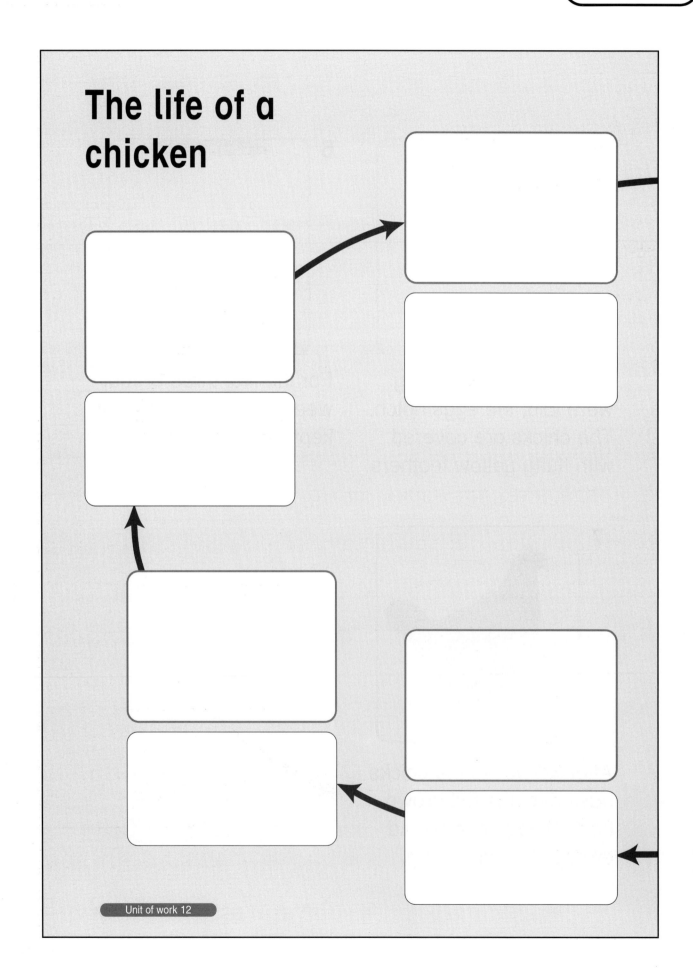

The life of a chicken

Unit of work 12

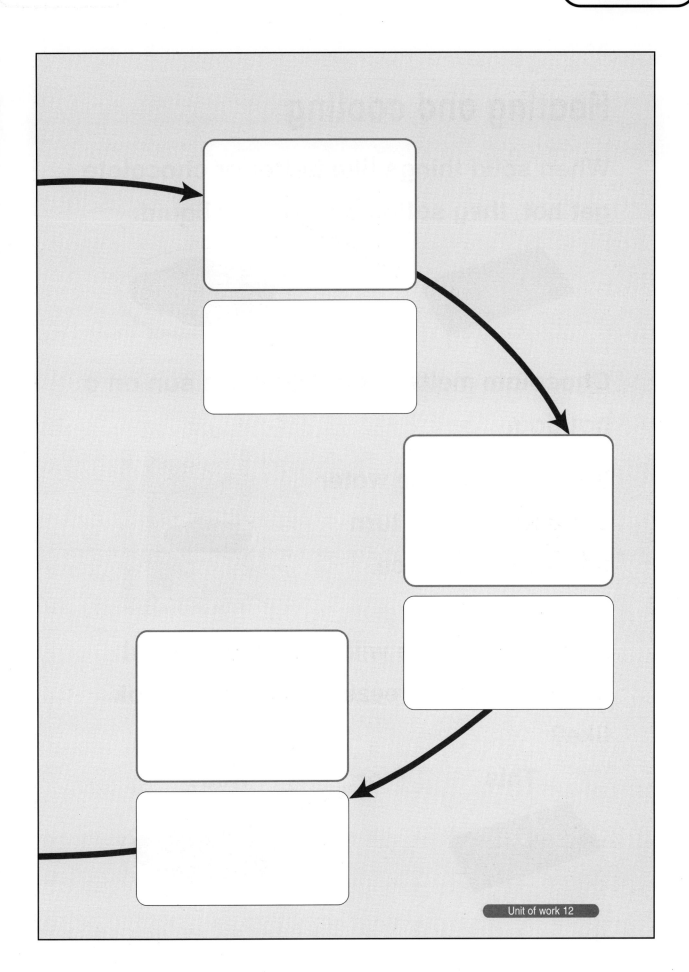

Heating and cooling

When solid things like butter or chocolate get hot, they soften and turn to liquid.

Chocolate melts if it is left in the sun on a hot day.

When liquids like water are cooled, they turn into solids, like ice.

Melted chocolate will harden if it is put into a fridge or freezer. What will it look like?

This   or   this?

Unit of work 13

Making a flow diagram

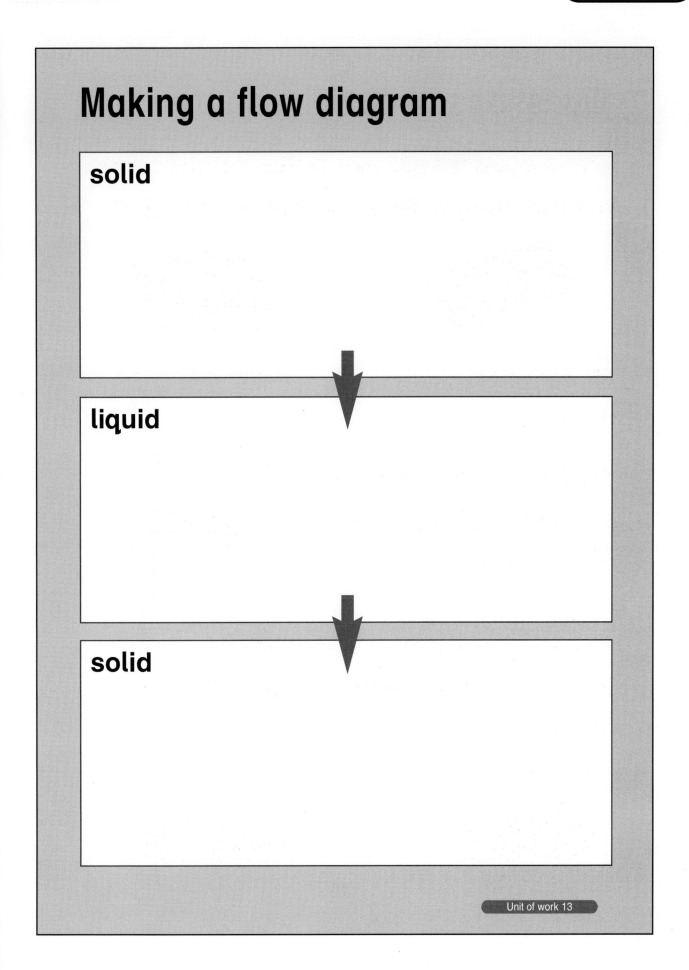

solid

liquid

solid

Pelican Shared Writing Non-Fiction Year 2 © Pearson Education Limited 2001

Questions about dinosaurs

Unit of work 14

Unit of work 14

The last dinosaurs

65 million years ago the last dinosaurs roamed the Earth. Some were plant eaters and some were meat eaters. For plant eaters it was easy to find food. Meat eaters had to hunt other dinosaurs, or look for the bodies of animals that had died. Plant eating dinosaurs often had horns to protect themselves from attack. They usually stayed together in herds. Meat eaters could use their speed to escape from danger. They often lived alone.

The Torosaurus

(pronounced tor – oe – sor – us)

The Torosaurus was a plant eating dinosaur that usually lived in a herd. It had the largest head of any dinosaur, with an enormous crest to frighten away meat eaters. It had huge horns to defend itself, and a heavy beak to tear down branches or dig up roots. It had flat teeth to grind up its food. A fully grown Torosaurus could weigh seven tonnes.

Units of work 15, 16 and 18

The Tyrannosaurus Rex

(pronounced ti – ran – oe – sor – us)
The Tyrannosaurus Rex was a terrifying meat eating dinosaur. It weighed up to six tonnes. It had a huge mouth with sharp teeth 18 centimetres long for ripping and tearing meat, and sharp claws on its tiny front legs for attacking its prey. It could eat up to 70 kilograms of meat with one bite! The Tyrannosaurus was good at hiding among trees, ready to leap out on its victim.

Units of work 15, 16 and 18

Dinosaur fact file: Apatosaurus (pronounced a–pat–oe–sor–us)

Appearance: One of the largest land animals ever (27m long, 15m tall). Long tail and neck. Nostrils on top of its head.

Weight: Up to 35 tonnes

Food: Plants

How it lived: Hatched from huge eggs 30cm wide. Probably lived alone. Lived for about 100 years.

Interesting facts: Had stones in its stomach to grind tough plants.

Fact file: Indian elephants

Where found: South-east Asia

Appearance: Rough grey skin. Long trunk. Small ears. Male elephants have tusks.

Height: 3 metres   **Weight: $5\frac{1}{2}$ tonnes**

Food: Grass, leaves, fruit, bark. Drinks by sucking water in its trunk, then shooting it down its throat.

Work: Used in forests for pulling and carrying loads of timber and in special processions.

Other interesting facts: Has a sensitive 'finger' on the end of its trunk. It can use this to pick up tiny objects.

Fact file: African elephants

Where found: Africa, south of the Sahara desert

Appearance: Rough grey skin. Long trunk. Large ears. Male and female have tusks.

Height: 4 metres   Weight: $7\frac{1}{2}$ tonnes

Food: Grass, leaves, fruit, bark. Drinks by sucking up water in its trunk, then shooting it down its throat.

Work: Not used for work.

Other interesting facts: The African elephant has two very sensitive 'fingers' on the end of its trunk. It can use these to pick up tiny objects.

Unit of work 18

Baby clothes

When grandparents were babies

Small babies wore nighties. The nighties were fastened at the back

Grandma

Grandad

with long tapes. Most babies wore terry towelling nappies.

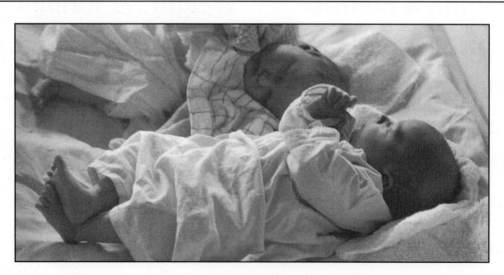
Nighties were made from soft, warm fabric.

Unit of work 19

1950s

Older baby girls wore dresses knitted from wool or made from pretty fabrics. Boys wore knitted jackets and leggings. Most baby clothes were in pale colours such as blue, pink, lemon or white.

Most mums could knit clothes like these.

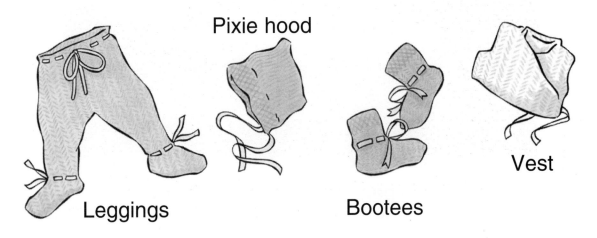

Pixie hood

Leggings

Bootees

Vest

Unit of work 19

When grandparents were toddlers

Boy toddlers wore short trousers. Girls wore dresses or skirts and jumpers.

Grandma

Grandad

Toddlers spent a lot of time in their prams.

Unit of work 19

1950s

The toddler is wearing a siren suit.

When children went outside they sometimes wore a siren suit. This was fastened by a long zip. Some clothes were bought from shops, some were made at home.

What babies wear today

Small babies today wear

Most babies wear

Older baby girls and boys wear

Most baby clothes are

Year 2 Non-Fiction Cross Curricular Links

	Unit of work	Topics covered	Links Pupils should be taught:
Term 1	1: Write directions	Maps and directions	(**Geography** G2e) to make maps and plans
	2: Use arrows and boxes		(G6a) the locality of the school ...
	3: Write instructions for a game	Instructions	(**Design and Technology** DT1c) to plan what they have to do suggesting a sequence of actions
	4: Order instructions in sequence	Writing a simple recipe	(DT3a) to talk about their ideas, saying what they like and dislike, identify what they could have done differently
Term 2	5: Use diagrams in instructions	Making a decoration	(DT2a) to select tools, techniques and materials for making their product, measure, mark out, cut and shape a range of materials (**Art** A4a) about visual and tactile elements, including colour, pattern and texture, line and tone
	6: Use appropriate tone for instructions	Making a den	(**Design and Technology** DT1c) to plan what they have to do suggesting a sequence of actions
	7: Make a dictionary	Dictionaries	(**ICT** 1c) how to gather information from a variety of sources
	8: Make a glossary	British wild animals	(**Science** Sc2 5a) to find out about the different kinds of ... animals in the local environment
	9: Use commas in lists		
	10: Use captions and headings	Toilets	(**History** H2a) about characteristic features of the periods ... studied
	11: Write simple sentences	Life cycle of a chicken	(**Science** Sc2 2f) that ... animals can produce offspring and that these offspring can grown into adults
	12: Draw flow diagrams	Effects of heating and cooling	(Sc3 1e) to recognise differences between solids, liquids and gases
	13: Use flow diagrams to explain a process		
Term 3	14: Write down questions	Dinosaurs	(Sc2 5b) to identify similarities/ differences between local environments and ways in which these affect animals and plants
	15: Make notes from texts		
	16: Write non-fiction texts		
	17: Use capitals and full stops in sentences		
	18: Write a report	African and Indian elephants	
	19: Turn statements into questions	Baby clothes past and present	(**History** H2a) about characteristic features of the periods ... studied
	20: Write non-fiction texts with headings		